All rights reserved. No part of this book may be reproduced in any form without written permission of the copyright owners. © Rebecca McFarland 2020

Hello Colorists!

Thank you so much for purchasing my coloring book. The pages of this book are inspired by my lifelong love of the female portrait, my daily walks in nature and the birds outside my window.

Knowing others were going to be coloring these pages filled me with joy as I drew them. I have been challenged, uplifted and inspired by each woman. As you enter their worlds, I hope you find relaxation and creative fulfillment.

I would love to see your colored pages. Tag me on Instagram @rebeccamcfarland or Facebook @artistrebeccamcfarland and let's connect!

If you would like to visit my website and see what else I'm working on, it is rebeccamcfarland.org

Thank you so much! Enjoy!

Made in the USA
Monee, IL
29 November 2020